MW01488039

T.A.L.K. Publishing
5215 North Ironwood Road, Suite 200
Glendale, WI 53217
talkconsulting.net
publishwithtalk.com

publishwithtalk.com

Title: **Why Your Brand Needs A Book**
ISBN 978-1-952327-32-2

why your BRAND needs a Book

JOLANDA J. ROGERS

Dedicated to every heart with a book inside of it waiting to be written. You have something to write that the world needs to read and until you write it, the impact of your written legacy is missing in the earth. It's time to unwrap the literary gift inside of you. If you're not sure how to do it or if you need support, I am here to take the journey with you.

Let's T.A.L.K.

Contents

Foreword

I remember the first time I heard the word brand and didn't think about my favorite laundry detergent, luxury car, slogan, or hotel chain. It was 2007, and I had just decided to send my pink Cadillac back to Mary Kay Cosmetics and start my own business. I was unfulfilled sitting behind someone else's desk. I still remember the day I met Ken, one of my mentors, for lunch. It was over lunch that he dropped a bomb on me when he told me that I needed to establish one.

"Establish a brand," I swear I walked around like a deer in the headlights for at least two weeks trying to figure out just what that meant. Lucky for you, you have this powerful tool written by the even more powerful JoLanda Rogers.

And while the book you've picked up isn't necessarily about branding, there are a few things you should know about this buzz word that is truly the key to sharing a powerful promise with those you want to lead, influence, impact, and transform. And the first is this....

Branding is the act of creating a powerful, compelling message and deploying that message through the medium [in this case, a book] that will produce the emotional connection your ideal target audience needs to decide to make a financial investment in themselves through you...

I know you can already see where I am going here, so let's get to it...

To continue with the story, after the two-week haze lifted, the first thing I decided to do was {wait for it} write a book.

Seriously. What better way to establish a brand than to write a book?

A book is a legacy establisher. For years to come, people will be able to read my story and shift. When I was ten years old, I made a powerful declaration at the urgency of Mrs. Dixon, my 5th-grade teacher, to channel my anger into writing. For two solid weeks, I wrote in the composition notebook she gave me as a desperate attempt to help me shift my anger and negativity after witnessing my mother taken to jail in a drug raid during my 8th birthday party. At the end of the two weeks, I returned to Mrs. Dixon, elated with a powerful declaration: I was going to use words to change the lives of others.

I'll admit that I didn't entirely know what that meant until the 9th grade when I met Jane McFann, a published author, and decided that my purpose was to use words to change lives in books.... Now, I also admit that after that startling revelation, I wrote nothing. Nada.

Instead, I got bogged down by life, graduated from college, and took a "good job" in corporate like most. And after 12 years at my good job, I left because sitting behind someone else's desk no longer served me, and I started my Mary Kay Cosmetics business. After finishing that second pink Cadillac, it was painstakingly clear to me that not only was I not living my purpose of using words to change lives, but I was also letting fear keep me from doing what I knew I must.

Once Ken told me over lunch that I needed to establish a brand, I realized this was my chance to finally do what I said I would. I went to work. I started on my first book, *If You Understood My Past, You Would Understand My Praise,* the very next day. I had learned that behind every "brand," there is a powerful story, and putting my very powerful story of breaking belief barriers into a book was exactly what I wanted to be known for in the marketplace.

Now, let's not get it twisted; a book is an expensive business card. It will open doors for you that will lead to bigger paydays, greater transformation, and the ultimate fulfillment of your life's work and purpose. However, the book itself isn't likely to cause a flood in your bank account. If, and that is a big if, you can silence your inner incredible snatcher, prove your family wrong, and proceed even if you feel fear you could write a book that is the beginning of the most profitable time in your life.

And so, with my knees knocking with fear, I decided that my faith was bigger, and I started on the journey to write the first of my now eight books. I felt in my spirit that people wanted to hear my story and wanted to know why I was challenging my own status quo by starting my own business, although I once had a "good" job. I knew when people understood your why, what you do has a greater impact, and I wanted to live my mission and purpose to transform lives. Truthfully, I was very clear:

the best way to share my why with the world was in my *own* book.

So, just like I hope you decide to do as you embark on this incredible journey with JoLanda; I started writing, and I didn't put my proverbial pen down until I shared the crux of my brand story in a way that would allow others to know me, like me, and trust me.

And the results? A Brand that is shaking the planet. That first book has turned into eight, plus powerful business systems, keynotes, television appearances, and a high-end coaching experience for my clients. In full transparency, writing that first book is why I am the CEO of a multi-million-dollar brand to this day.

As you continue to think through the best way for you to tell your brand's story, remember that your voice is worth sharing. There are people right now crying themselves to sleep in the same predicament you made it out of. They literally just prayed for a sign that everything is going to be all right. Imagine their delight when they get to read your story of how you turned lemons into lemonade, developed a powerful framework, solved a serious problem, or whatever you did to turn their tears into triumph. That is the power you possess with your brand, and that book is one that the world can't wait to read...what are you waiting for?

Your brand needs a book! Get to writing - we are waiting for you and your book to establish a written legacy that will impact generations.

Darnyelle Jervey Harmon, MBA
Incredible One Enterprises
www.incredibleoneenterprises.com

Your Brand is Worth a Legacy

Let's begin by being very clear on who I'm addressing in this short but life-changing book. If you're an influencer, speaker, counselor, coach, pastor, business owner, or survivor, *Why Your Brand Needs a Book* is for you! If you can categorize yourself by any of the above titles, then chances are you have a brand. If you don't, you need one. Your brand is what sets you apart. It makes you unique and easily identifiable. Let's play the brand game for a moment. I'm going to list a few famous slogans, and I want you to think of the brand associated with them. Ready? Go.

- Just Do It.[i]
- You Can't Eat Just One.[ii]
- Can You Hear Me Now? Good.[iii]
- Think Different.[iv]
- I'm Lovin' It.[v]

More than likely, as you read each of the above slogans, you had imagery enter your mind as well. You could picture the words because the brand is vastly known and associated with who they are and what they do. It is an unconscious association of what you've heard, seen, and felt by reading the words. We hear the slogan or tagline, see the logo, experience the product — and ultimately drives us to support the brand.

Why Your Brand Needs A Book isn't a book about branding, so I won't spend a lot of time there. However, it's an important point to note that knowing your brand matters. Who are you? What do you represent? What do people know you for? How do they feel when they encounter you? How do they feel when they leave you?

I strongly recommend that you have a clear brand strategy as you approach writing your book. Some of the most successful books are associated with a "brand," and brands are associated with "people." Yes, bestselling authors are brands, and people know them by their books' genre (their brand).

In the examples provided, some person was the initial brainpower behind the launch and start of a multi-million-dollar brand that began as a thought in that person's mind. That's who I'm addressing in this book, the person behind the multi-million-dollar brand (that would be you). I need you to see beyond cash flow and see into the value of what you do and who you are. In fact, if you do that, then we are not talking about a million-dollar brand – we are talking about a priceless brand. Your priceless brand deserves a legacy.

If you've invested your heart in building a brand, you know the money, time, commitment, coaching, marketing, and fierce determination to sustain a brand in a heavily brand saturated culture. Having a book (of substance) is one way to set your brand apart and create a legacy for your brand that no one will soon forget.

Think about the common assumption when communicating business — "if it's not in writing, it doesn't exist." Heard that before? The last thing I want for you is to have a brand, have a story, make a transformational impact on the world, and not leave it somewhere in writing.

Your brand deserves a legacy. It deserves to exist long after you're gone. You deserve for it to exist long after you're gone. So I'm going to make what I'll call a "stretch" analogy, but follow me. What if the Bible had not been "written" down? For the pastors and leaders of faith that will read this book, did you know there are 63 relevant bible verses about writing? I'll share my top five in case a biblical reference will encourage you to give your brand the book it deserves. The other reason for sharing these five powerful verses is that I pray as you read them, purpose will arise in you, compelling you to **write the book**.

> **Jeremiah 30:2** (KJV) Thus speaketh the Lord God of Israel, saying, Write thee all the words that I have spoken unto thee in a book.

This isn't a biblical study reference book, so don't judge my interpretation, okay? But it sounds obvious to me that God is saying to Jeremiah that there is a book already written inside you. Write the words I have spoken to you! As a publisher, we use this concept as one of our foundational principles to structuring our writing process. The book is already written. Your commitment is to surrender to the process and write it out. Other translations of this verse state to "write in a book for yourself." Write for yourself spoke to me that first of all, your brand needs a book for _you_.

Psalm 45:1 (NKJV) My heart is overflowing with a good theme; I recite my composition concerning the King; My tongue is the pen of a ready writer.

Where are my survivors and life dominators? I'm speaking to the people reading this book, which by all justifiable causes should not even be here to read this book, let alone think about writing a book. Your life is a good theme; you have a story worth sharing. More importantly, a soul is waiting to read your survival as a testament that what you've survived; they can survive as well. I'll also attribute this verse to the speaker whose brand needs a book. Your tongue is the pen of a ready writer. Do you understand the powerful impact of that statement? You are speaking the words that need to be written. Your book is already done! We will address some of the barriers that block the words from your mouth, becoming chapters in a book later. For now, your tongue is a pen. Wow!

I hear you; you don't consider yourself a "writer," but are you a talker? Then let your tongue do the writing.

Habakkuk 2:2 (KJV) And the Lord answered me, and said, Write the vision and make it plain on tablets, that he may run who reads it.

Habakkuk opens this chapter by sharing he is standing and waiting to hear what God will say to him. In his listening, he heard that he must write the vision. God commanded him to write them plainly on tablets so that those around him could *run* and move forward based on the words they read. Their forward movement was contingent on him writing what was given to him by God. I wonder if you are reading this book and you are a coach or a counselor, and there is a written word in you that someone needs so that they may run. Meditate on this: they cannot run without the vision, and they can only receive the vision if you **write** it.

Job 19:23 (NKJV) Oh, that my words were written! Oh, that they were inscribed in a book!

Again, where are the survivors of LIFE? Even if you fall into one of the other categories as a coach, counselor, pastor, influencer, or business owner, the likelihood is that you are also a survivor. Where are the multimillionaires who people see where you are now, but they have no idea what you've gone through to reach where you are? Your book is more meaningful than rags to riches. It is the fuel for somebody's fight to live another day.

The business owner who almost quit on day 937, and because you kept going, on day 938, you hit growth in your business that changed your entire life trajectory. I need you to know that other business owners are approaching their quit day, and your book will be their saving grace.

Job was going through it! (please hear that in a very passionate voice because that's how much he was going through) Even in that, he follows this verse by saying I know that my Redeemer lives! What have you gone through and **survived**? Every reader of this book has a testimony of survival to write.

Psalm 102:18 (NKJV) This will be written for the generation to come, that a people yet to be created may praise the Lord.

Did that spark something in you the way it did in me? Your Brand is worth a Legacy! It is bigger than you, but it needs you in order to manifest. There is more in this book, and I want you to keep reading, but we could settle on the answer to why your brand needs a book with this scripture alone. You are writing for people that have yet to be created. Think of literary influencers that are no longer living but have written books and spoken words that have shaped your life.

One of the most powerful quotes that have shaped my life is by the late Maya Angelou. She would speak with such passion and conviction that "there is no greater agony than bearing an untold story inside you."

Why your brand needs a book? So the agony of bearing what you've always wanted to say, what you've needed to say, and what the world needs to hear – can finally be released. Breakthrough the wall of unspoken and unwritten words; free yourself.

The Top 5 Barriers Between You and Your Book

As a publisher, I am aware that there are several reasons those that should write — don't.

After consulting monthly with hundreds of aspiring authors whose brand really deserves a book, I've compiled the top five reasons people talk themselves out of writing their legacy.

> #1 I'm not a good writer.
>
> #2 I don't have the time.
>
> #3 It's too much money.
>
> #4 Everyone is writing a book now.
>
> #5 I don't have anything to say.

BARRIER #1 - I'M NOT A GOOD WRITER.

Let's start with the first barrier that also happens to be what I consider a primary excuse because there are so many reasons around this said "barrier." <u>I'm not a good</u>

<u>writer.</u> The first question I ask aspiring authors when confronted with this barrier is, who told you that? Who said you weren't a good writer, and what was their level of influence that it has so stifled the gift inside you to release the words that are already written?

When aspiring authors engage in a dialogue with me about writing a book, 99% of the time, they've thought about doing it and have secretly desired to do it for years. I'm always perplexed at the reality that one person's opinion of who someone is as a writer (or not) is loud enough to silence their words. If this lie has ever been a barrier for you, consider asking yourself who told you that, evaluating their influence, and deciding if their words are still true to you.

Once you make this evaluation, you will conclude that their influence is not more vital than the message inside you that the world is waiting to read. I hope that the opinion of those who do not matter is not greater than the influence your book can have to save someone's life (literally).

When it comes to being a good writer, the other aspect to consider is who makes the decision here? Is it you, your readers, old voices? If this has been a barrier for you, how did you make this determination regarding your ability?

My guess is that if you've never written a book, then you don't have millions of readers telling you you're not a good writer. You've never been added to the Tomatometer for books (yes, that's a thing), but you're not on it. And guess what? If you write the words that are already written inside you, with the confidence that the world is waiting to read them — you never will be.

Assessing the "goodness" or quality of your writing can only really be understood when you identify precisely who you're writing to and exactly what they need to read. Once you've identified what I like to call your *perfect reader*™, write to them and trust me – they will see your writing as not only good but great!

Hang on, before you think I'm dismissing the obvious, I'm not. When the phrase "good" writer is used, it's also attributed to English mechanics. I overstand this fact. By <u>overstand</u>, I get it, and yes, there are varying levels of writing skills. Your writing skills and quality of content are not the same things. The two are often confused and sadly merged, resulting in million-dollar manuscripts never making it to the paper because the writer doesn't consider themselves a "good" writer.

We live in the beautiful age of technology, and with that comes countless programs you can purchase or use for free that can support you in English mechanics. Some programs can do a high-level spell check and necessary grammar review. More extensive programs will look at your clarity, engagement, delivery, sentence structure, consistency in content, and even PLAGIARISM. If the barrier of being a "good" writer results from the words an 8th-grade English teacher proclaimed, there are resources to eliminate this excuse.

BARRIER #2 - I DON'T HAVE THE TIME.

I'm always intrigued when I hear <u>I don't have the time</u>, because having "time" is relative to where we want to spend it. Actually, if we are spending time, we are losing time, as the well-coached phrase is to "invest time," not spend it anyway.

Can I use the word <u>*overstand*</u> again here? I'm hoping you said yes, because as a mom with multiple business lines AND a publishing house, I understand the value of time and how precious it is. I also understand that there are somethings worth investing your time in because it will yield a timeless return.

Creating a book for your brand is worth the time investment. Again, we live in an age where there are creative ways to meet your goals. So perhaps, sitting down in front of a computer for hours is unrealistic for you. Have you considered having someone transcribe your book for you? Transcription is an amazingly quick and effective way to get the book that's written inside of you out into the ears of someone who can put it on paper.

There are multiple ways to do transcription. You can speak your book out into a platform that will transfer your words to text, or you could hire someone to transcribe as you talk.

If you are a speaker, pastor, coach, or influencer, the likelihood is that you have tons of verbal speeches, talks, and sermons that are already books! Your next step is hiring someone to bring together what you've said into literary form. Don't assume that if people "heard" it, they aren't interested in "reading" it.

Remember, there are various learning styles, and there is a place for your book among those that enjoy seeing, feeling, and reading literary art. Not everyone will attend the large event or watch the replay, some souls still need your content, and it will be received best if done so through a paperback or e-book.

BARRIER #3 – IT'S TOO MUCH MONEY.

Following closely behind barrier #2 is barrier #3. <u>It's too much money.</u> Is it really? Let's consider where and how we spend money. Money, like time, is an investment, and if you are just "spending" it, you probably don't have enough of it because you don't understand it's value.

You will get what you pay for in most cases. So am I discouraging you from using an inexpensive publishing company to get your message out? Yes. Please do your research, find out what they've published, and find out how successful their authors are after they've published.

If you are a top-earning professional in your lane of service, I think you'll agree with me that the world should know about it, right? Right. Darnyelle Jervey Harmon (multi-millionaire coach and writer for the foreword of this best-selling book) says it best — "a book is an expensive business card." It can create opportunities for you to broaden your reach and expand your territory in making the world aware that your brand is worth recognizing!

Very quickly, let's switch from English and play around in the math department. There are 365 days in a year unless it's a leap year. A delicious venti drink at Starbucks with extra pumps of your favorite syrup and a double shot of espresso can quickly add up to $8.00 per drink. Of course, drinks go best with a sandwich or pastry so add $5.

$8 + $5 = $13 per day

$13 per day x $365 *days per year* = $4745

That's almost $5k in breakfast for a year. I'm also pretty sure that you share with your friends, and often "drinks are on you," so if we triple that, you have almost 15k spending, not investing but spending on breakfast. I also did not add the cost of waiting in line (your time) or your gas to get there.

Did you know that you can enroll in a quality publishing program starting at 10k? You can, and I'll tell you about that later.

BARRIER #4 – EVERYONE IS WRITING A BOOK.

Let's move to barrier #4. Everyone is writing a book. I remember so well being asked as a child, "if everyone jumps off a bridge, will you jump off the bridge?" Of course not, right? However, this isn't a bridge, and we aren't talking about doing what's trendy. We are talking about doing what's purposed. If you know that your brand deserves a book (and it does), then it doesn't matter who else is writing a book! The reality is they aren't writing YOUR book.

I am known for not going with the status quo; I just prefer to be different, stand out, and express my uniqueness and individuality. I've never believed in doing something because everyone else is doing it; therefore, I wouldn't encourage you to write a book because everyone is doing it. My imploring to write a book that your brand deserves is because I genuinely believe your brand deserves a book.

One of the questions I ask aspiring authors is how long they've contemplated writing a book? For many of them, the answer is years, sometimes decades. If this is you, what are you waiting on?

Another aspect of barrier #4 I must address is the notion there are too many books in your genre or about your topic. It doesn't matter how many books are about your topic; until you've written your book, those words haven't been written. Period.

Just as unique as each person is, that's how unique books are. No two people on the planet share the same experiences, and even when they do, they don't experience them the same. The outcome is a different story because you have a unique value different from anyone else in the world.

When you stepped out to launch your brand, open your business or start your church, you didn't say, "well, there are too many churches in the city, I won't open mine." No, you knew there was something different inside you the world had not seen, and it needed exposure to your gift. Knowing you have a gift and that you are a gift is essential. If you truly understand your brand and know your secret sauce's value, it will be easier for you to understand why it deserves a book.

Let's make it even more relevant; for those that have children, according to Worldometer, there are 7.8 billion people on the planet.[vi] In a desirable situation, when you

31

found out that you or your partner was expecting, I am pretty sure you didn't think, "well, there are so many people already on the planet, it doesn't make sense for us to add another one." You celebrated the coming arrival of your baby because you knew that it was love expressed through a divine creation, and it didn't matter how many people were on the planet at the time; your baby wasn't here!

When you see that baby (for emotionally healthy parents), you don't see them as one in 7.8 billion. You see them as the only baby on the planet. Even if you have more children, they each have a special and unique place in your family, and although raised by the same parents, they are entirely different. In the same way, you see that child as deserving a place in destiny regardless of the 7.8 billion people already here; your brand deserves a book regardless of the number of books already written. Yours has not been, and it deserves to be.

I believe that each person serves an intended purpose, and no one can do what you can do, the way you do it. Take two life coaches, for example; they can use the same program and follow the same process, but because of their uniqueness as individuals, each coach will produce

different results for their clients. It also depends on the client that is being served as well because no client is the same. I'm over-explaining because many people are resistant to releasing what's inside them out of fear that the market is oversaturated.

Until you've said it your way, it hasn't been said, and until you share your story, it hasn't been shared. More importantly, a perfect reader™ is waiting to read *your* book. They are waiting on the message that you will release, and it doesn't matter how many books they've read; until they can digest the written words from your soul, they will not move into the life created for them. Your perfect reader™ is waiting.

BARRIER #5 - I DON'T HAVE ANYTHING TO SAY

Finally, to barrier #5, <u>I don't have anything to say.</u> This barrier is often a silent internal struggle that has also come from something somebody told you. If you reflect on barrier #1, not being a good writer, thinking you don't have anything to say deserves the same intimate reflection to identify where the voice came from and who spoke those words to you directly or indirectly.

If it was something you heard early in your formative years, this might be a place you need to spend intentional time exploring. You do have something to say. Even if you didn't say it in a book, even if you didn't have a brand that deserves a book – you have a voice that deserves to be heard and acknowledged.

Barriers to fulfilling our purpose can often have deep roots. When it comes to really knowing your value and worth, the origins are often hidden in memories and experiences that aren't even in our active awareness. If you've ever recited the words "I don't have anything to say" in your head, it came from somewhere. I'll leave you to dispel that lie and receive the truth where you need it. Not only do you have something to say, but you also have something to write that someone in the world is waiting to read!

Your brand has a story, and there is something to be written about how your brand came to be. Even if you stumbled into the beauty, you now behold as your brand, what caused the stumble? How did you encounter divine alignment to strategically cause you to live the blessings your brand has created? I promise you have more to say than what you realize and once it starts flowing, watch out! You may find a new purpose in translating your passion to text. What begins as your brand needing a book becomes a captivating literary journey that leaves a mark on the world that lasts forever.

When you reach heights in business and life that others see as making it "there" or what "success" looks like, you may appear superhuman. People may assume you don't put your pants on one leg at a time or that you've never experienced the pitfalls of life. You can lose that personal touch that connects people with your brand essence. Giving your brand the book it deserves is a way to connect people with the person behind the brand. You have so much to say, and I'm confident that people are waiting to read it because of how valuable your brand is. They want to hear from you.

Brake through the barriers! Bust out of the mental blocks separating your brand from the book it deserves.

#1 You **are** a good writer!

#2 You **do** have the time!

#3 It's **not** too much money!

#4 No one has written **your** book!

#5 You **do** have something to say!

What Your Brand Is Missing by Not Having a Book

Having a book adds value to your brand, and believe it or not, your brand is *missing out* by not having a book. Writing a book can take you from having business experience to becoming a business expert in your lane, both literally and figuratively.

You literally become an expert in your brand because of the investment you will make into creating a quality book. Whether you do this through ghostwriting or writing your book yourself, it will involve some form of research, reflection, and collecting resources to develop meaningful content. As you go through this process, you will emerge as an even more profound expert in your brand. It will be necessary to look at what makes your brand unique and what set's you apart. The more you do this, the more effective you will become in properly articulating your brand to your prospects and the clients you serve. You will become immersed in your why, and it will seamlessly flow into the lives of those connected to your brand.

You figuratively become an expert because you've *written* a book! We talked about barriers and listed one of them as being everyone is writing a book. So listen, while this is a barrier, it is only partially true. Not everyone is willing to invest in writing a book. If they were, I wouldn't have written this book to remind powerful world changers like you that the world is waiting on your words.

Giving your brand the book it deserves sets you apart because while many begin books, not everyone finishes their book. There are always more starters than finishers. If you've been in business any amount of time, I'm sure you know this to be true from peers and pop-up shops you've seen around you. Everyone that started with you hasn't continued. You are missing out on your expert status literally and figuratively by not giving your brand a book. Claim your status! You deserve it. You've earned it; now put it in writing.

The most frequently asked question about my business initially was "what do you do *exactly*"? As a business with multiple service lanes, I found that my books helped bring brand clarity to those seeking my services. I've written books in each service lane of my business, and I've used them to connect with my ideal clients and share the message and purpose of my brand. Becoming an expert in my business and about my brand, both literally and figuratively, has drawn clients to me that I was missing out on at first because they needed clarity around the services I offered.

Guess what? This book is one of the books I created because my publishing brand needed a book! It's so amazing, it deserved a book, and I couldn't deny it the recognition or expansion it craved because it is a life-changing brand! I want you to think the same and believe the same about your brand and know that it yearns for expansion!

Consider all the hard work you've done and your investment; you wouldn't have a gorgeous outfit and leave it in the closet forever, would you? Would you purchase a classic or custom car and never drive it? At some point, you'd take it out on the town and enjoy the blessing your brand has afforded you. Give your brand it's night out on the town through developing a book the world is waiting on.

Did you know you are missing out on **expanding** your brand market by not having a book? I was recently a contributing author to an anthology that reached 15 countries in its initial distribution. My market grew overnight, *literally*. My brand grew from recognition in 4 countries to recognition in 15 countries through an opportunity to contribute to a book. I am positive that some amazing people will read this book (thank you, by the way). As impressive as you are, you cannot be in 15 countries simultaneously; however, your book can. Your brand is missing out on connecting with the world in ways you physically cannot at one time.

Even if your brand requires you to travel and have opportunities to speak across the country, your brand is missing out on creating an even further reach by not having the book it deserves. There are ways to tap into international book markets to get your message out beyond your neighborhood. My brand and my book will reach people and places I may never physically come in contact with, but my message will. The most profitable brands are more significant than the people that created them. Think big about your brand. It's okay for it to be bigger than you – it's supposed to be.

I will invite you to learn how your brand and your book can build your bank at the end of this book, but very quickly, I want you to know that your brand is missing out on money! You are leaving money on the table by not writing a book for your brand. Will you get rich off of book sales? Maybe not, BUT you can create opportunities from your book that can produce multiple streams of income. You can't reach this new market of revenue if you don't write the book.

There is a confidence and sense of accomplishment that 100% of authors report feeling after their book is complete. Knowing that they started and finished a lifetime achievement gives their brand extra swag and sets them apart from others in their field. You are missing out on knowing what this feels like! Let me tell you, as an author, it is rewarding to know that you've invested the time, dedication, and the will power to finish a book.

Your brand needs a book because once you have one, it cannot be taken away from you, and it is something that you will forever receive recognition. Products come and go; they change, they increase and decrease in popularity.

Books have longevity in the market. As long as there are time and space, there will **always** be a place for a book in your brand. It will never get old or go out of style.

Your Perfect Reader™ is Waiting

Perhaps one of the most important reasons I believe your brand needs a book is that your perfect reader™ is waiting. I've mentioned this a few times already, but I want you to get it. I want you to understand the value of your message to the person that's waiting on it. Have you ever needed to connect with someone or something, and when it happened, everything made sense? I want you to know that your book can have a powerful influence on someone's life in this same way.

Understanding the urgency of your perfect reader™ waiting makes me think of the parable of the starfish project. The parable talks about an older man who walked along the beach, picking the starfish up and throwing them back into the ocean. Thousands of starfish were in the sand, and they were dying. The starfish could only survive if they were in the ocean. An observer noticed him picking up each starfish one by one and throwing them into the ocean. He questioned the man as to why he was wasting time picking each one up.

The man explained that if the starfish stayed out of the water too long, they would dry out and die. This person informs the man that there is no way he would be able to pick up all of the starfish and throw them back into the ocean before it got dark. He tried to convince this man that his efforts didn't matter, and what he was doing did not make a difference. In his wisdom, the man picked up another starfish, and before throwing it in the ocean, he said, "it mattered to this one."[vii]

Here's my version of the starfish parable; I call it the author's story. It is an aspiring authors conversation with Doubt while the perfect reader™ waits:

An aspiring author sat in the bookstore where he dreamed his book would one day be. Thousands and thousands of books were around him, row by row, shelf by shelf. He observed all of the books written by other authors. While gazing at the literary art, a person by the name of Doubt walked up beside him.

"Why are you staring at all the books in this bookstore?"

The author responded, "Because I'm writing a book, and one day, my book will be alongside the other books here in this store for the perfect reader™ to find it."

Doubt responded, "But don't you know everyone is writing a book? There are thousands of books already in this store; you can't possibly believe that adding your book will make a difference. Even if you finish your book – who will buy it?"

The author listened and pointed ahead, noticing a reader looking aisle by aisle for the perfect book. Browsing each title, they picked it up and put it away. That was not the right book for them.

The author responded to Doubt and said, "Do you see that reader over there? The one who can't find the perfect book to speak to their heart and provide the inspiration they've been looking for?"

"Yea, so," Doubt replied.

"That is my perfect reader™, and they are waiting for my book. There isn't a book in this bookstore to speak to them the way mine will, and until I write the book I've been created to write, it hasn't been written. I must write —for that one."

Your brand needs a book because you must write to that <u>one</u> who has read all of the other books about your subject. The one who has experienced brands similar to yours, but they have not received what they need because what they need is *you*.

They need to read your book. Something in them needs a literary connection with you. There can be a deep connection between reader and author without the two ever meeting.

Recently I had a chance to hear one of our authors share about her book at a speaking engagement. She talked about how, while writing her book, she felt *swallowed* by her past pain. She described her process of healing and building a brand that is nationally recognized. During her talk, the author shared her past pain shaped the future direction of her life and her business. At the end of the event, there was an opportunity to purchase autographed copies of her book. She sold out of her books at that event.

While at the signing table, her perfect reader™ approached her with tears in her eyes. The reader shared that she had never been able to explain the feeling her past had on her, but when she heard how this brand leader felt _swallowed, she could immediately identify._ She had to have the book because not only did she identify with the sentiments of the author, but hearing her speak and now holding her book was the strength she needed to find her voice.

Your perfect reader™ is waiting, and they need you. I shared this author's experience and her perfect reader™ because when your brand has a book, you can leave a tangible piece of who you are with those connected to your brand. Think about it; your brand is not limited to a small group of people. Even when people hear our message and experience us, they often need something to remember us after we're gone. Leaving your perfect reader™ with a book that reflects your brand creates a connection with them that stays forever.

You physically leave their presence, but your book creates a place for them to return and connect with you whenever they want to. Talk about brand accessibility; give your perfect reader™ unlimited access to you through your book. They can return again and again.

Powerful Brands With Powerful Books

By now, I hope you see why your brand needs a book. I hope you are stirred enough to realize that you need to explore the next steps. In this book's opening, I shared with you; my goal to address the influencer, speaker, counselor, coach, pastor, business owner, and survivor. Now that you've been addressed, I want to share with you powerful brands in each of these categories that were bold enough to give their brand the book it deserved.

Influencer: Edward Hennings, author of The Answers: A Guide to Passing the Test of Your Life

Speaker: Nancy Yarbrough, author of The Exodus: Where New Beginnings Happen

Counselor: Dr. Lisa Sinclair, author of Restoring the Paths: Sexuality for Christian Leaders

Executive Coach: Robert Pyles, author of Anchoring the Big 6: Proven Strategies to Transform Your Life

Pastor: Darryl Seay, author of Radical Faith: Learning to Trust God Radically

Business Owner: Dionne Grayson, author of The Making: Trust God to be the Chairman of Your Boardroom

Survivor: Maria Fonseca, author of Alone but Not Alone: Discovering God's Light in Dark Places

Learn more about their brand and their book on the following pages.

Influencer

Edward Hennings — *The Answers: A Guide to Passing the Test of Your Life*

In Edward's book, he discusses how his life's most significant test came when a judge sentenced him to forty years in prison for first-degree reckless homicide. He details how it forced him to reconsider the legacy and impact he wanted to leave as a man.

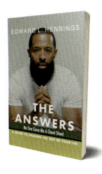

You'll have to purchase his book to get the details, but from his emerging brand came his book. Edward served twenty of his forty-year sentence, and within three years of his release, he built a brand with multiple streams of revenue. He is now a sought-after speaker, curriculum developer, and execution coach under Eric Thomas and

Associates. His book is endorsed by one of the largest prison systems in the nation, housing over 23,687 inmates, all of who have access to The Answers because Ed gave his brand a book.

Edward didn't stop with his book, his brand continues to grow with a trucking company, a beard oil product that came from his passion as a barber, a life skills curriculum based on his book, and he was signed for a book tour to share his brand and his book with his perfect readers™.

Edward is a change agent in ending recidivism and coaching aspiring business owners with a less than perfect past on how to transfer their street skills into business skills. In 2020 he launched The Change Institute, and you can find him under the hashtag change is the new hustle.

#changeisthenewhustle

#theanswersbyed

#changeinstitute

Purchase Ed's book at edwardhennings.com. It is also available on Amazon and Barnes & Noble.

ARE YOU AN INFLUENCER?

If your brand has the power to sway your target audience to follow your lead, the answer is probably yes. Influencers motivate people to make a guided change based on their industry knowledge and credibility. If your brand has an influence that produces sustainable change for your clients, it needs a book.

Speaker

Nancy Yarbrough — *The Exodus: Where New Beginnings Happen*

Nancy is a nationally recognized speaker and advocates for eradicating human trafficking. A survivor herself, she founded Fresh Start Learning, Inc., a non-profit with a mission to strengthen families, restore the underprivileged people of society, and rebuild communities. By advocating and raising awareness of social justice, her organization strategically creates social development programs to transform survivors' lives.

Nancy had a booming brand! On top of that, she is also the TEDx speaker of Myths, Misconceptions, Mysteries, and Mistakes of the Sex Trade. Nancy had a well-recognized brand in her areas of influence. She now has a book that goes before her, creating new invitations and opening multiple doors for her brand to increase impact, influence, *and yes,* income.

After writing her book, Nancy developed a processing station for her perfect readers™, facilitating author talkbacks. She's created a healing movement from trauma and destructive cycles by giving her brand a book the world was waiting on.

Nancy is known for proclaiming, "No more suffering in silence." Her impact has reached thousands of survivors and transformed numerous lives. Nancy is a prime author to explore when you think of what makes your book successful. Various measures define success, and she has written one of the most successful books in addressing her perfect readers™.

Learn more about Nancy's organization Fresh Start Learning Inc., and consider donating to further a healing movement at freshstartlearninginc.org

Purchase your copy of The Exodus: Where New Beginnings Happen at nancy-theexodus.com.

Nancy's book is also available on Amazon and Barnes & Noble. If you know of survivors healing from experiences within human trafficking, purchase a book to share with them.

ARE YOU A SPEAKER?

If your brand is associated with your voice because people are inspired when you speak, the answer is probably yes. If you speak from a pulpit, conference room, lecture hall, or small group, your brand deserves a book that represents the power in your voice! Especially if you've been fortunate enough to speak before audiences of 500+ or platforms such as TEDx. I encourage you to consider having a book to leave with your audience, allowing them to savor their experience with you.

Counselor

Dr. Lisa Sinclair — *Restoring the Paths: Sexuality for Christian Leaders*

As a sought-after international teacher on grief and trauma, Dr. Lisa Sinclair wrote a book that further established her as a subject matter expert. Within the first week of release, it received a request for multi-lingual translations. Lisa is a psychiatric nurse practitioner, missionary care consultant, and international speaker. She bravely translated her passion and burden to help global church leadership discover the balance of Christ's grace and truth in sexuality.

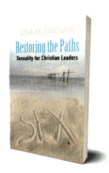

Dr. Sinclair's recognition as a trusted voice was validated across the world by endorsements from notable influencers.

"Lisa Sinclair has addressed a vital issue in a comprehensive manner gracefully but straightforwardly, with erudition and compassion, outlining a principled stand and offering practical steps forward."

Stuart Briscoe

Pastor Emeritus at Elmbrook Church

Milwaukee, Wisconsin

Founder of Telling the Truth

"Dr. Lisa Sinclair has addressed a serious challenge the world is experiencing. She has studied, researched, and provided divine wisdom from the Bible to enable the restoration of God's design for sexuality."

Dr. Paul R Gupta

Hindustan Bible Institute & College, India

President

Through consultations, workshops, and seminars, Dr. Sinclair shares her expertise in sexuality and wholeness, transcultural teams, conflict management, and mental health and trauma. She gave her brand a book, and as a global counselor, she created an extension of the gift she is to stay with those around the world even when she isn't physically in their presence.

Purchase your copy of Restoring the Paths: Sexuality for Christian Leaders by visiting www.lisamsinclair.com Lisa's book is also available on Amazon and Barnes & Noble.

ARE YOU A COUNSELOR?

If you are a Licensed Professional Counselor, Wounded Healer, Soul Care Provider, or your brand establishes you as a resource to guide individuals dealing with concerns affecting their mental health and wholeness, your brand needs a book. There is a high probability you've developed a technique, have a particular message, or a concept to share with your perfect readers™ that will transform their lives because of your gift. Gather your years of experience and passion for healing and give your brand the book it deserves and *needs*.

Executive Coach

Dr. Robert Pyles — *Anchoring the Big 6: Proven Strategies to Transform Your Life*

Dr. Robert Pyles is an Executive Coach. He is also a multi-million dollar restaurant franchise owner, real estate developer, author, pastor, husband, and father. You will often hear him share; he is the same guy, with the same goals, serving the same God in whatever environment he's in. He empowers his clients through experience, not theory that being anchored in six critical areas guarantees exponential success.

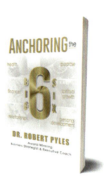

Anchoring the Big 6 is based on health, finances, relationships, spiritual growth, personal development, and purpose. Through his coaching programs, he demonstrates how Anchoring the Big 6 is not to challenge your dreams; it's to make your dreams last. With a reputable and multi-lane brand, Dr. Pyles did not stop at one book; he has published several books and builds out his content strategically to address the areas in his coaching program. In anchoring your relationships, he has a companion book titled I Love My Wife But, I Love My Husband But. Both books aim to remove the but out your marriage and embrace your husband's or wife's personality as a gift.

Dr. Pyles has been recognized on the list of America's Largest Black-Owned Businesses. To purchase books or become a client in his coaching programs, visit rpthebig6.com, where you can anchor the life you deserve. His books are also available on Amazon and Barnes & Noble.

ARE YOU AN EXECUTIVE COACH?

If your brand is reputable and you have proven through experience, not only through a theory that you can produce transformation in the lives of those you serve — your brand needs a book. The difference of transformation through a theory is that you haven't actually experienced it, so you are only telling others it's true because of what you've heard or read. To become a reliable Executive Coach, it's imperative that you've experienced what you promote as effective. Your perfect reader™ will know the difference.

Pastor

Darryl Seay — *Radical Faith: Learning to Trust God Radically*

Pastor Seay is a sought after preacher, presenter, consultant, and lecturer. He has served as an adjunct professor at the Impact School of Leadership in Milwaukee, Wisconsin, and has more than 25 years of ministry experience. As the senior pastor of Liberty and Truth Ministries, he serves a growing multicultural ministry changing lives through God's word. The ministry thrives through biblical kindness, radical hospitality, lament and hope, and trauma-informed ministry.

Besides his ministerial credentials, he also holds a master's in Counseling and Student Personnel Services and is pursuing his DMin.

For many spiritual leaders, your ministry is much more than just what happens inside the four walls of your church. Pastor Seay is also the LTM Freedom Center Founder, where the mission is to see individuals and families living in wholeness, personally, financially, professionally, and spiritually. They offer a clothing closet, food pantry, computer lab, job assistance, housing assistance, and AODA support.

As a pastor, instructor, business owner, and community influencer, Darryl Seay has hundreds of books in him. His brand as a pastor and respected lecturer has provided him the opportunity to capture his content and his message in literary form. His first book Radical Faith: Learning How to Trust God Radically, was in his arsenal for years before releasing it.

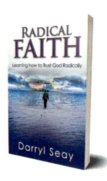

In his book, he chronicles Abraham's life with practical life principles to increase your faith walk. He doesn't shy away from his personal story while doing so; his perfect readers™ get to know him not only from his position

behind the pulpit but through his journey as a man, husband, and father.

His commitment to release his first book can now fuel the release of other books through sermons, study guides, curriculums, and more. As a pastor and frequent speaker, most of his content is already written! To purchase his book and receive divine inspiration and encouragement, visit ltmmke.com

ARE YOU A PASTOR?

If you are a Pastor, Spiritual Leader, Evangelist, Elder, a person who has committed your life to faith and encouraging others to do the same, you already know there's a book in you. The conversation for you is not about if you'll write — but when you'll write. Your message is the extension of your faith, bringing comfort, healing, and refuge to those who will read it. Give your ministry the book it deserves.

Business Owner

Dionne Grayson — *The Making: Trust God to be the Chairman of Your Boardroom*

Dionne Grayson is a Business Owner. She is also a woman of faith who used her first book to share her entrepreneurial experience with the wisdom she's acquired by allowing the Holy Spirit to guide her in her business endeavors.

In her first release, The Making: Trust God to Be the Chairman of Your Boardroom, she explains your boardroom is a sacred place. It's the intimate conversations and quality time spent with God that guides your decision making.

Dionne challenges her perfect reader™ by asking them, are you allowing the Holy Spirit to have His say? Through her experience, she confesses you can receive the best business counsel from your Board of Directors or industry experts, but when it is time to decide what to do and implement what you know, the counsel of the Lord must stand.

By sharing daily business encounters parallel with David's life and ministry in the Bible, her perfect readers™ discover how posturing themselves as David did in the Bible will bring success as you navigate business decisions, challenges, and wins each day.

Dionne Grayson is the Principal of Building Your Dreams, LLC. With more than 25 years of partnering with individuals and empowering others to live their life on purpose, the Milwaukee Business Journal recognized her as a Woman of Influence. She was in O, The Oprah Magazine, Fortune, and Entrepreneur in the Leading Women in Business section. Her calling is to equip others to manifest their destiny by confidently walking in purpose. She earned an undergraduate degree in Clinical Psychology from Alverno College and a graduate degree in Social Work Administration from the UW-Milwaukee.

Dionne launched out to give her brand the book it deserved and realized that there was more. She is preparing to release a goal-setting journal and a children's book series centered on finding and following your purpose, by design — not by default.

To purchase her books and learn more about her mission and business, visit themaking.store or buildingyourdreamsllc.com

ARE YOU A BUSINESS OWNER?

Do you own a business where you serve others, or perhaps sell a product, have a non-profit, or a unique gift you've used to leverage your brand? What keeps you going? How did it all start? Great businesses aren't born overnight. Even if the world knows what you do, giving your brand the book it deserves will share with them why you do it. When it comes to marketing, people hardly buy your what. They are always willing to buy your why.

Survivor

Maria Fonseca — *Alone but Not Alone: Discovering God's Light in Dark Places*

Maria Fonseca is a poet, advocate, abuse survivor, and author. She is on a mission to bring awareness to childhood sexual abuse and the spiritual, emotional, and mental brokenness it leaves behind. Her message is to bring hope to adult survivors for healing and freedom through a relationship with Jesus Christ. She lives in Chicago but enjoys exploring other parts of the world. She is a mother and grandmother.

In her first book, she shares a powerful story of healing from childhood trauma and has used her book to share her brand message that God can heal trauma and that He was present during the trauma. Maria's book has grown into a blog, garnered television and radio appearances, and allowed her to create opportunities to share her message through workshops and seminars.

In Alone but Not Alone: Discovering God's Light in the Darkness, she asks the challenging question, "If God is good, where was He when the abuse happened to me?" She eloquently shares trusting in God's goodness is a difficult challenge for sexual abuse survivors.

Armed with biblical truths and a vulnerable heart, as a childhood sexual abuse survivor, she invites you to join her as she revisits the dark places in her life where she exposed the lies she believed about God and discovered truths about his presence, protection, and plans for her.

Maria leads her perfect readers™ on a journey to discover God's light where they know in their darkest moments; they were never alone. She describes how:

- Loyalty to culture and family can enable secrecy.
- Sexual abuse distorts perspectives about God.
- Mental illness is often spiritual brokenness that can be healed.

- Forgiveness frees you.

To purchase her books and learn more about Maria, visit mariafonsecawrites.com

ARE YOU A SURVIVOR?

Have you overcome a significant life event or trauma and have a desire to share your story through a message of healing, hope, and survival? Have you found yourself in one of the other categories, but you also know that there is a story that fuels your passion and pushes you into your brand purpose? Own your narrative, share your voice; your brand deserves it — and you do too. Write. The. Book. There is a perfect reader™ that has a similar experience, and they don't know what survival looks like. They long to heal, but they aren't sure where to start. Your book could be the words they need for hope and wholeness.

5 Things You Must Know to Write Your Book

It wouldn't be fair of me to tell you that your brand needs a book and not tell you the five things you must know to write your book. Whenever you approach a literary journey, I believe it is necessary to keep your perfect reader™ in mind, and as my perfect reader™, I wanted to offer you the gift of the five things you absolutely must know:

1) What type of book are you writing?
2) Who needs to read your book?
3) What's the purpose of your book?
4) What qualifies you to write a book?
5) How will your book serve you and your perfect readers™?

WHAT TYPE OF BOOK ARE YOU WRITING?

In the literature world, there are two primary categories and a plethora of literary genres. The two categories are fiction and non-fiction. Fiction books are generally written from a creative lens of fabricated content. Non-fiction books are based on truth and facts. Below are a highlight of fiction genres and non-fiction genres, but to get the best detail of each genre, head over to jolandarogers.com, and you can download the details of 30+ genres for free in the expanded version of 5 Things You Must Know to Write Your Book.

Fiction Genre Examples

Action & Adventure

Crime & Detective

Drama

Fairy Tale

Humor

Romance

Short Story

Non-Fiction Genre Examples

Autobiography / Biography

Devotionals

Journalism

Memoir

Poetry

Religious Text

Self-Help

WHAT TYPE OF BOOK ARE YOU WRITING?

In this book, you've noticed me reference the perfect reader™ frequently. I do this because just as a successful business targets a preferred audience for marketing, you must target the perfect reader™ for your book. You want to have a clear understanding of what type of person will benefit from reading your book. As you are writing, you will write with them in mind.

For example:

1. Are you writing a self-help book for single mothers?

2. Is it a collection of short stories for the avid reader?

3. Is it a memoir for individuals who are on the verge of giving up on their dreams?

It works best if you define your perfect reader™ as much as possible. You want to know everything about them, how they feel, what they think, what they need.

Identifying your perfect reader™ will create a solid marketing strategy for selling your book. Once you know who your perfect reader™ is, find them, and make that your advertising platform. You want your advertisements visible where your perfect reader™ can see them. You'll need to decide if they spend most of their time on Facebook or LinkedIn, do they prefer Instagram or Twitter?

Identify them, find them, love them, write to them and for them.

WHAT'S THE PURPOSE OF YOUR BOOK?

Independent of the category or genre, there should be a clear reason for writing your book. Did you identify with any of the authors shared in the previous chapter? Are you a speaker, influencer, counselor, pastor, business owner, executive coach, or survivor? You may find your purpose in the lane you most identify.

Books are written for various reasons, and if you have a brand, the primary reason for writing is that your brand deserves a book. Here are other purposes books serve:

Describe: Share something with your perfect reader™, such as the details of a particular event or experience. (Survivors)

Educate: Provide information on a particular topic or share content to improve a perfect readers™ life. (Executive Coaches)

Encourage: Give hope and support to a perfect reader™. (Pastors)

Explain: Make a concept clear to a perfect reader™ that will give them a more in-depth understanding. (Counselors)

Inform: Reveal facts, information, or perhaps offer instructions to a perfect reader™. (Business Owners)

Inspire: Compel a perfect reader™ to feel passionate toward a particular subject or content. (Speakers)

Persuade: Offer a perspective or a call to action that will provoke a perfect reader™ to respond. (Influencers)

You'll notice I indicated where a particular brand might find a purpose for their book but in no way does this limit your scope. Often books serve more than one purpose. The key is to know the purpose and be confident you've accomplished the purpose by the end of the book.

WHAT QUALIFIES YOU TO WRITE A BOOK?

Am I even qualified is a question writers think internally and seldom asked out loud, so I'll not only ask the question — but I won't leave you hanging without an answer.

So many influential people live behind a wall of unspoken words. I know because I was one of them. As powerful as my voice is, and despite the impact and influence I evoked everywhere I went, there were still words unspoken. By breaking through this wall of unspoken words, I realized it was the barrier between me and my next income milestone, between me and true emotional freedom, between me and everything I secretly desired but was so afraid to go after. Why Your Brand

Needs a Book is a call to not only speak the words but to own them and write them for your perfect reader™.

Everyone has a story to tell, and something to share that can benefit another soul. Therefore, the very thing that qualifies you to write a book is your desire, personal life experiences, and knowledge. The truth behind writing a book is, in most instances, it has very little to do with your economic status, educational attainment, accomplishments or lack thereof, career field, etc.

Writing a book is about sharing your story in whatever genre and purpose that fits you. Since it is YOUR story, no one else can write it the way you can. It's kind of like having that secret where you know something no one else does. The difference here is that what you know and what you have to share, *people are longing to hear.*

There is a world of perfect readers™ waiting in expectancy for what's inside of you. Why keep them waiting?

If you have a brand, do you really want your brand's longevity to depend on someone maintaining it for you, or do you want to give your brand the book it deserves, which is something no one else even needs to maintain because writing it makes it permanent?

I went back and forth with this book's title between Why Your Brand Needs A Book and Why Your Legacy Deserves A Book. Both are true, and all you need to do is write; right now.

HOW DO YOU WANT THIS BOOK TO SERVE YOU AND YOUR PERFECT READERS™?

Your book has the potential to transform your life and the lives of your readers. Can you define how? To answer this question, you will most likely need to gather and organize your thoughts. You can start with pondering and answering the following questions: *(Note: all questions may not be relevant for your book)*

1) What realistic expectations do you have for the book?
2) What doors would you like opened for you after writing the book?
3) What's your primary topic or theme?
4) What are your key points, principles, ingredients, characters, components, ideas, etc., that you want to convey?

5) How do you want the reader to feel while and after reading your book?
6) What do you want the reader to do after reading your book?
7) What do you want the reader to know after reading your book?

Writing and publishing a book will be one of the most rewarding things you will ever do in your life. It is an accomplishment worthy of praise, and your book can have a significant impact on your personal and professional life.

Giving your brand the book it deserves can:

1) Grow your platform
2) Produce viable streams of income
3) Establish you as an expert in your industry
4) Create a tangible product to leverage your brand

The opportunities from writing a book are limitless.
- JoLanda Rogers

81

Why I Gave My Brand the Book It Deserved

It was important to me that I not only share this message, but I live this message. My publishing brand deserved a book. I am the proud CEO of a brand that has produced authors who generate viable income streams from the books they've published with us. Our authors own their rights and royalties. Two things that are my company's core values because no one has the right to own a story you've lived. It isn't just about having a good book; it's about honoring the stories of those brave enough to write the book.

A few years ago, I set out to publish traditionally. While opportunities were presented to me, I could not settle down and commit. It was challenging to know there was a possibility, my voice and story would be drastically modified, and I would need to ask permission to use my story in ways that I rightfully deserved. At the very least, I felt I deserved to own the rights to the content that has fueled my passion and propelled my purpose. I encourage all writers to read the fine print of publishing contracts and look for two main components 1) ownership of your content 2) the percentage of your royalties.

Writing a book and sharing your story, experience, and knowledge will require time and effort, but it is well worth it. Like most things, it's easier if you don't have to do it alone. Therefore, I want to share my commitment to take the journey with you through one of our signature publishing programs at T.A.L.K. Consulting, LLC.

If you are reading this book, I know that you are my perfect reader™. I also know that means there is a book inside of you that you need to write. For whatever reason, you haven't written it yet — that's okay, you can write it now.

At T.A.L.K. Consulting, we understand that writing a book is not only transforming for your perfect readers™ but writing a book transforms you. During this transformation process, you'll need community, a coach, strategies, and all the tools to finish your book without stress and overwhelm; that's precisely what we provide.

Contact us for a free consultation on our secret sauce to write, print, and publish your book in 90-days.

Visit jolandarogers.com to join the conversation and give your brand the book it deserves.

Your Brand Deserves A Book, and so does Your Legacy.

T.A.L.K. Soon

Join the Conversation

Stay Connected to JoLanda
www.jolandarogers.com
www.publishwithtalk.com
www.talkconsulting.net
myauthorlab.com
Facebook: @talkconsulting1
Facebook: @JoLanda Rogers
Instagram: @talkconsulting1
Twitter: @talkconsulting1
LinkedIn: @JoLanda Rogers

Contact JoLanda
wepublish@talkconsulting.net
262.477.3100

More Books By JoLanda
- Today Will Be A Great Day Vol. I
- Today Will Be A Great Day Vol. II
- A Pocket Message to Survivors of Childhood Sexual Abuse
- A Pocket Message to Responders of Childhood Sexual Abuse
- A Pocket Message to Perpetrators of Childhood Sexual Abuse

- Yours is Yours & Mine is Mine – When It's Okay Not to Share (children's book)

Contributing Author
- Blessed is She: The Transforming Prayer Journeys of 30 African American Women
- 7 Day Journey to Discovering Your Purpose: God's Vision, My Hands. Partnership With the Divine.
- Lotus Legal Untold Stories Survivor Magazine

References

[i] https://nike.com
[ii] https://lays.com
[iii] https://verizon.com
[iv] https://apple.com
[v] https://mcdonalds.com
[vi] https://worldometers.info/world-population
[vii] https://positivelifebalance.com/blog/star-fish-beach/